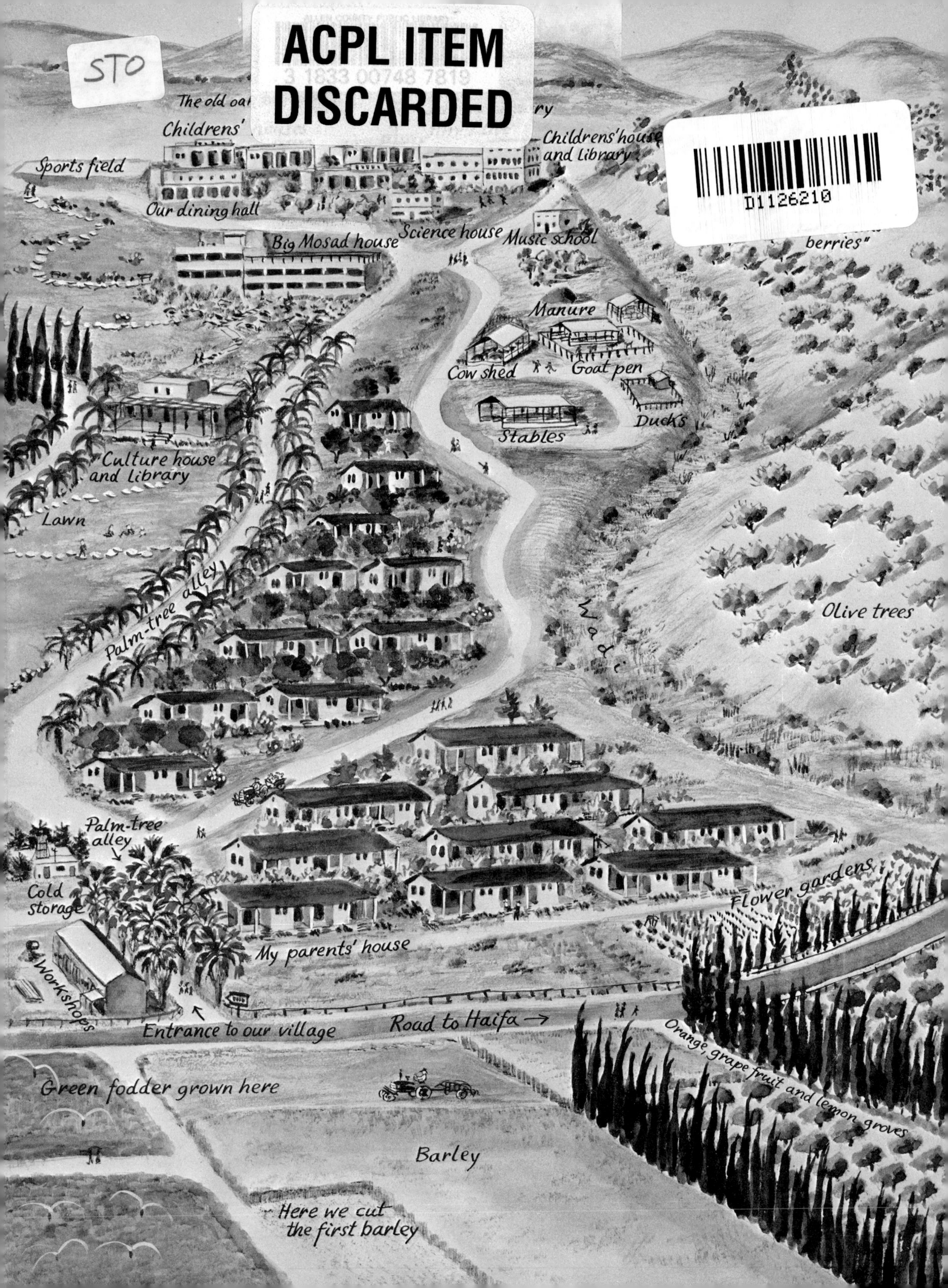
Childrens'
Childrens' house
and Library
Sports field
Our dining hall
Big Mosad house
Science house
Music school
berries"
Manure
Cow shed
Goat pen
Stables
Ducks
Culture house
and Library
Lawn
Palm-tree alley
Wadi
Olive trees
Palm-tree
alley
Cold
storage
Workshops
My parents' house
Flower gardens
Entrance to our village
Road to Haifa →
Orange, grape fruit and lemon groves
Green fodder grown here
Barley
Here we cut
the first barley

BY THE SAME AUTHORS

My Village in Austria

My Village in India

My Village in Ireland

My Village in Yugoslavia

My Village in Norway

Follow the Reindeer

MY VILLAGE IN ISRAEL

by Sonia and Tim Gidal

PANTHEON

 / PUBLISHED BY PANTHEON BOOKS INC., 333 SIXTH AVENUE, NEW YORK 14, N. Y. / LIBRARY OF CONGRESS CATALOG CARD NUMBER: 59-8591 / PRINTED BY THE MERIDEN GRAVURE COMPANY, MERIDEN, CONNECTICUT / MANUFACTURED IN THE U.S.A.

1

My name is Shmuel. I live in a village in the land of Israel, on the slopes overlooking the Emek, the Valley of Jezreel. It is called the Guardian of the Emek. My father, Chaim, and my mother, Ruth, were born in Poland. They came here thirty years ago, together with many other pioneers, and founded our village. But I was born in Israel, and so I am called a Sabra, which is also the name of the wild cactus that grows all over our country.

I live in the Mosad, the children's community of our village. All the boys and girls over twelve live here. It is a real complete village inside the big village.

We have our own houses and our own school in the Mosad, our dining hall and big kitchen, our own animal farm with cow shed and horse stable and sheep pen and goat pen. We have vegetable gardens and orchards, and even our own fields.

It is six o'clock in the morning. I am waiting up here on the cactus hill for my cousin Adam and my friend Uri. Adam is still in the library in the big white building down below. I asked him to take a book back just to keep him out of our way for a few minutes—because Uri and I want to play a trick on him. The three of us sneaked out of our rooms before the others got up. Uri and I told Adam to meet us at the Sabras up here and we would show him our secret cactus tree.

I live in the second house to the right of the library, just behind the shed. There are four bedrooms and one big classroom in each house, and in each bedroom live four children. The sixteen of us from the four rooms learn together in that big classroom. We are all about the same age, around twelve.

When my parents came here, there wasn't a single tree on our hills except the old oak tree and the olive groves. But every year since then the villagers planted thousands and thousands of trees, and now there are more than a quarter of a million trees in our forest. Our chief forester is Emanuel, the father of my friend Uri. Emanuel has planted more trees than anybody else, and he says that he knows every tree personally.

From our village I can look across the Emek, the Valley of Jezreel, to Mount Tabor and to the hills of Nazareth. Many battles were fought in the valley, even back in ancient times. And when I was a baby my father and my mother and the other villagers fought there too. They defended the village against a big invading army of Arab soldiers from Syria.

The Arabs set up artillery on the hills around us and shelled our village. Most of our houses were full of big holes. Before the attack came, I and the other smaller children were evacuated to a safer place near the town of Haifa. But my brother Yuval and my sister Hagar, who were both more than ten years old, stayed and helped as runners, and looked after the animals. My brother's best friend was killed by a bullet just when he was milking the ewes. What a terrible time that must have been! But in the end the villagers drove the enemy back to Syria. It all happened the year our State of Israel was established, in 1948.

Now I can see Adam climbing up the slope on all fours. Adam only arrived from Poland two months ago. His mother and my mother are sisters. My cousin does not speak much Hebrew yet, but he can already understand quite a lot, if you only speak slowly to him. Adam is a little stingy with his belongings. He brought his bicycle from Poland, and of course everybody wants to ride it because we don't have any bicycles ourselves. But you can ask Adam for days and he won't lend you his bike—he keeps it locked up with a chain!

Imma—that's what I call Mother—says we should leave Adam alone and give him time to get used to our way of life, where all of us share everything. But we still want to show him, and so Uri and I have decided to play a prank on him. Uri is over by the cactus already, and he is sticking goat droppings on the sharp thorns. We collected the small, hard balls in the goat pen before we climbed up here.

"Come here, Adam!" I call. This is a warning signal to Uri, and he stops his work.

"There is our secret cactus tree," I tell Adam.

"Look at the beautiful berries," Uri says. "You can take a few to show to the Nature teacher, Adam. But don't *eat* any of them, I am sure they are poisonous."

"Yafeh, yafeh," Adam says, "beautiful, beautiful," and he picks a few of the goat droppings from the thorns, holding them carefully in his hands.

Uri and I sprint down the hill, but Adam walks slowly, protecting his precious berries.

"Maher, maher," I call back to him, "hurry, hurry—or we'll be late for school!"

We didn't wash today and we skipped morning exercises, so we would have time to sneak up to the hill, but we must not be late for school. The first period starts at seven o'clock. We are in our seats just in time, everybody else is there already.

They have been giving us tests for the last two days. Yesterday they were on the Bible and on Ancient Greece, the day before it was arithmetic and botany. Today is our last morning in school and the last test. Tomorrow we go on a trip to the ancient fortress of Megiddo. The day after tomorrow Pesach begins, and that's the start of our spring vacation.

Teacher Ezra hands out the sheets of questions. Adam has gone to a special Hebrew lesson instead of taking the test; it would still be too hard for him. Uri takes Adam’s seat next to me, but when we think of the surprise Adam will get from his rare berries we start to giggle, and that annoys the teacher. He changes places with Uri—because we disturb the class, he says—and he sits next to me.

I make a face, because I am not happy with the change. The teacher sees it, and points to the inscription on the wall. We made the wooden letters for it in the workshop and hung them up there. They read: HACHAVER L’MAAN HAKVUTZAH—HAKVUTZAH L’MAAN HACHAVER: The Friend for the Group—The Group for the Friend.

Today’s test has thirty questions. I start with the easy ones:

Name the countries bordering on the Republic of Israel. I fill in the answer without trouble: North—Lebanon. East—Syria and Jordan. Southwest—Egypt.

Name the water boundaries. West—the Mediterranean Sea. East—the Salt Sea (also called the Dead Sea). South—the Red Sea.

Name the longest river. The Jordan River. It flows through Israeli territory for seventy-three miles.

Tell what you know about the Salt Sea. The surface of the Salt Sea lies about 1300 feet below sea level, it is the lowest depression in the world. It is called the Salt Sea because its water contains more salt than any other sea in the world—there is one part of salt to three parts of water. Many chemicals like bromide and potassium are taken from the Salt Sea by evaporating the water in shallow ponds. No fish can live in the Salt Sea, and for this reason the Greeks called it the Dead Sea.

What is a tell? A tell looks like a hill with the top chopped off. Inside it are the remains of ancient towns, each built on the rubble of the previous one. There are over four hundred tells in Israel. Forty of them have already been excavated, for instance the Tell of Megiddo.

We always have breakfast after the first school period. I hand my test to the teacher and run over to the dining hall.

I help myself to lots of shamenet, sour cream, and cut in scallions and tomatoes and sweet green peppers. I mush it all up properly before I start into it. Then I eat a hard-boiled egg and some bread and butter, and I drink hot chocolate with it. Now I feel better and can talk about the test. My cousin Loga sits opposite me.

"Did you mention that the Dead Sea Scrolls were discovered in 1947 near the Dead Sea, Shmuel?" she asks. "And that the salt makes the water so heavy you can float on it, even if you don't know how to swim?"

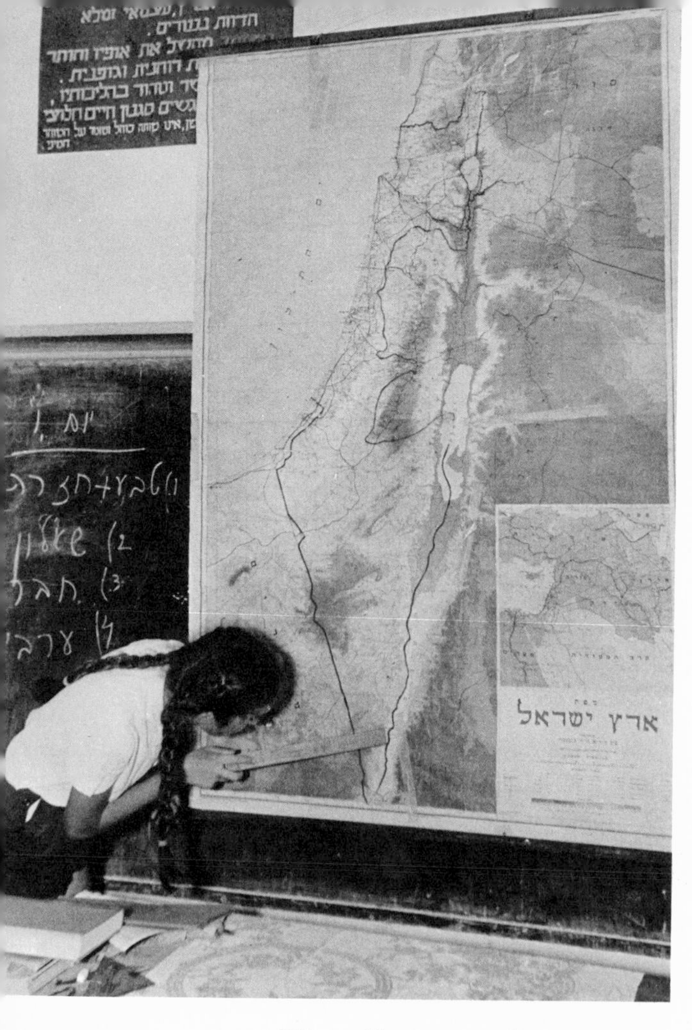

I get very mad at myself. About the swimming I don't care, it is not very important. But to forget the Dead Sea Scrolls! I know all about these ancient Hebrew writings. They were written two thousand years ago and were found in those caves in the wilderness of the Dead Sea shores.

Well, it is too late now, I can't get the test back.

We go to the classroom again. We now have a Bible lesson, again with Ezra. He tells us that there will be only one more period today instead of the usual five, because the agricultural manager had asked the children of the Mosad to help prune the plum trees.

We will miss Arabic today, and English, and Nature Study, and Arts. But we will make the lessons up one day during our vacation.

Adam sits next to me.

"Listen, Shmuel," he whispers, "how can I show the teacher the rare berries if we don't have a Nature class today? They smell funny."

"I'll tell you later," I answer.

"Quiet please!" says Ezra and looks at us. "Open your Bibles to Deuteronomy. Remember, we talked about the times the ancient Hebrews came to the frontiers of Canaan, almost forty years after Moses had led them out of Egypt. Now you read on, Amram. Start with chapter 8, verse 7."

Amram reads: "For the Lord your God is bringing you into a good land, a land of brooks of water, of fountains and springs, coming forth in valleys and hills; a land of wheat and barley, and vines and fig trees and pomegranates; a land of olive trees and honey; a land

in which you will eat bread without scarcity. You will not lack anything in it. A land whose stones are iron, and out of whose hills you can dig copper . . ."

"Stop right here, Amram," says Ezra. "Where are the copper hills Moses was talking about?"

Elisheva raises her hand: "It must have been in the Wadi Araba," she says, "in the desert rift between the Gulf of Aqaba and the Salt Sea." She goes to the map and points out the region.

Ezra asks another question. "How do we know there was copper in the Wadi Araba?"

Almost everybody raises a hand, and Loga is allowed to tell the story: "Some years ago a famous American archeologist named Nelson Glueck made excavations in the Wadi Araba. He found smelting furnaces and refining plants for copper. And then he found the copper mines too, farther up in the valley. The same copper mines that had once belonged to King Solomon. Here they are." And she points them out on the map. "And now those ancient copper mines are being exploited again," she continues, "and modern smelting furnaces have been installed there."

"Right, Loga," says Ezra. "Now you, Adam. We talked about Moses leading our forefathers from Egypt, where they were oppressed, to this land, where they became a free people. Ever since then, we celebrate the Exodus from Egypt. Do you know what we call this festival?"

Adam says slowly: "The name is Pesach, and it will begin in the evening of the day after tomorrow."

We read on in the Bible, and we talk about the meanings of the words and about the sentence structure.

When the period is over we rush out, and I take my books to my room and start to clean my trumpet.

Outside I hear bursts of laughter. Adam is standing on the verandah looking very stupid while the others howl with laughter. He has shown them his "rare berries," and now he is telling how he got them.

"That was a bad joke to play on anyone, Shmuel," says my cousin Loga when I join them, "and especially on a newcomer!"

"Ein davar, ein davar," Adam murmurs, "no matter, no matter."

"Uri and I wanted to tease Adam a little because he never lends us his bike," I defend ourselves. But Loga is really angry.

"Fine friends you are," she says. "Adam just came up to us and said he doesn't mind any more if we ride his bike. Here, look, he gave me the key for the lock, you *tambl!*"

Tambl isn't a compliment. It means a blockhead, but I think I deserved it, and now it is I who have the red face. I apologize to Adam.

"Uri and I got mad because we thought you were stingy," I say.

"Ah, ein davar," he answers. "Ein davar, you tambl!"

"You don't have to learn Hebrew *that* quickly," I say. "Can I ride your bicycle now, Adam, please?"

He takes the key from Loga and gives it to me. I pedal slowly past the verandah of our house, and then down the palm-tree alley.

At the dining hall Dollek is just sorting letters and newspapers into the mail rack by the entrance. He is the postmaster of our village. After he has stuck the mail into the small boxes, the villagers come to pick it up. Opposite the mailboxes hangs the daily work schedule for the chaverim, the friends, as the villagers call each other.

"What do mine eyes see!" Dollek jokes. "Humble Shmulek on Adam's bicycle. Not by power shall you gain a ride on this bike, but by sweet persuasion—how did you manage it?"

"Adam lets us use his bike now, and he offered it all by himself," I say while leaning it carefully against the house.

"Ah, the walls of Adam's selfishness have crumbled before the sweet trumpet sounds of friendship. Glad tidings indeed, glad tidings!"

When Dollek jokes, and he jokes often, he uses big words. We all like him very much. I must not forget to tell Adam Dollek's goulash story. That was a very funny one.

In vacation time the children of the Mosad eat with their parents in the big dining hall. Everybody takes turns at dining-hall duty, even Mordechai, who is a cabinet minister in the government, and Jacob, who is a member of the parliament. They spend a great part of their time in Jerusalem, the capital of our country.

One day, when Dollek was waiting on tables, he said to us:

"Oh ye multitudes, we have goulash yotzeh min haklal today, goulash extraordinary! May I serve you a fullness thereof?"

Everybody asked for a big helping. But what was so extraordinary about the goulash was that it was made of vegetables—with no meat at all!

Since then, any meal we don't care for is called "yotzeh min haklal —extraordinary."

Dollek has a second job: he is our weather man. Every day he works with four older boys and girls at our meteorological station. Together they compile the weather report and send it to the main station in Jerusalem. And they give the daily weather forecast to the village council.

"Dollek, did I get a letter?" I ask.

"It is my pleasure to inform you that there is such a one for you," Dollek answers, and hands it to me.

"From Yuval!" I shout, and rip the envelope open. "He says he is coming home for the Pesach days. Oh, he will be here in a few minutes—he's coming on the ten o'clock bus!"

"Verily, what else do you expect of a red-capped sky jumper," says Dollek. "It is his job to come unexpectedly."

My brother Yuval is a parachutist in the Army. And because the parachutists wear red berets, they are called Red Caps. But now I see my group passing by on the village lawn.

"Shalom, Dollek," I say, "we are going out to the plum orchards, to help with the pruning."

Shalom means peace, and we use the word to greet each other.

"Shalom, Shmuel," Dollek answers, "tell your friends they may eat as many plums as they like today, by extraordinary permission of your friend Dollek." I catch on, and call back:

"We will bring you some as a present." Dollek knows very well that we couldn't eat any plums today. They won't be ripe before June, and if we ate them now we would only get upset stomachs.

I tell my friends what Dollek said, and we all laugh a lot. But then I remember Yuval's letter.

"I will catch up with you," I tell my group. "I have important news. Yuval is coming. I have to run over to the dressmaking shop and tell my mother."

I open the door to the sewing room. Imma is just cutting out some cloth for shirts. She looks up and sees the letter in my hand.

"Is Yuval coming?" she asks, even before I can say Shalom.

"He will be on the morning bus!"

"Wonderful, wonderful!" the others in the workshop call out. "Quick, Ruth, go and meet your son—the bus is due in a few minutes."

They talk as if their son was coming home. I leave the workshop with Imma.

"Shalom, Imma," I say, "we are pruning trees today!" And I run after my friends.

2

At the edge of the plum orchards I catch up with my friends.

"Yuval is coming, Abba," I tell my father, who is already waiting for us. I always call my father Abba, and he mostly calls me by my nickname, Shmulek.

Abba is in charge of the work in our orchards. We have more than thirty thousand fruit trees: apples, pears, plums, apricots, avocados. Besides that we have almond trees and vineyards and large orange groves.

Abba has another job as well: he is the head librarian. We have eleven thousand books. Most of them are in Hebrew, but there are many in English too, and in Polish and Russian and German. Our parents come from many different countries of Europe, and most of them speak two or three languages.

"We have more fruit than we need, and fewer books than we want," Abba is in the habit of saying. "Therefore we sell fruit to buy books; that is our economy." This is his favorite joke.

The library is in the basement of our new culture house. On the ground floor is a big reading room, with magazines from all over the world, and chess tables, and a record player. Here we have concerts and lectures, and art exhibitions are also held in this hall.

The plums are still as small as olives, and green and hard, but they hang on the branches in thick clusters. There are far too many, and they take nourishment away from each other, and have no space in which to grow properly.

Abba supervises us and tells us what to do.

"Wherever you see the plums squeezing each other, pluck at least one out of three and throw them on the ground," he says. "The earlier we prune our plum trees, the better our Santa Rosa plums are in the end."

"Why are they called Santa Rosa? It isn't a Hebrew name," Loga asks.

"No, it is not," Abba tells her. "This variety comes from the United States, from the Santa Rosa Valley in New Mexico. It's the finest plum in America. And it so happens that our climate here in the Valley of Jezreel is similar to the climate of New Mexico. The Santa Rosa plum likes our climate, and so it grows very well here."

There are fifty of us children helping, and in two hours we finish the work for the day.

"Thank you, my friends," says Abba. "You have been a great help."

On the way back we pass the vineyards. My sister Hagar and four other women and girls are at work there. Hagar sits on an orange crate and binds the shoots with string up on the wires.

I know this vineyard very well; here we grow the Queen of the Vineyards, the best grape we have. The grapes get very big, and in the fall, when they are ripe, they are tasty and sweet.

Hagar wears a wide straw hat to protect her against the strong sun. These straw hats are the latest fashion in the village. Even some of the young men wear them. They say the straw hats are practical, but I think they just like the way they look in them. My old-fashioned tambl hat is practical enough for *me*. Sometimes I wonder who thought to name a hat after a blockhead.) Abba and all the other people wear it, it's practical enough for them too.

"Hagar," I call, "Yuval is here."

"Fine," Hagar answers. "What does he say, the jumper?"

"How would I know?"

"Don't give me a silly answer, tinok," says Hagar. "You said he's here, so you must have talked to him."

"In the first place, I have *not* seen Yuval. And in the second place, don't call me tinok. Call your tinok, tinok!"

Tinok means baby, and just because I was Hagar's baby brother once she has no right to call a grown boy silly names!

"All right, all right, I made a mistake," Hagar says, "and I beg your forgiveness, Shmulek. But how did the news reach you that our brother arrived?"

"He *wrote,* he wrote to *me!*" I answer.

I run after my friends, but I am stopped by Arye. He drives sheep and goats to the fields; he calls to me:

"Shalom, Shmulek, come here!"

We have hundreds of sheep and hundreds of goats, and we have three shepherds for them. One flock grazes in the fields in the Emek. The second climbs the hills, and the third flock wanders around in the woods.

"Are you bringing your goats from the Mosad today or tomorrow?" Arye wants to know.

"Tomorrow, Arye." The goats from our children's community are always brought to the big village pens during vacations because at that time we often go on hikes and can't take care of the animals.

Arye goes on with his flock, and I go my way, back to the village.

"Hoop! Get in there, you stupid cow!" I hear someone shout. It is Meir, feeding the cows in the open shed. He adjusts an iron bar so the cows can stick their heads through and get at the fodder.

Meir is in charge of our two hundred cows. He used to have ten helpers, but now he does most of the work by himself. Only two years ago, Meir and his helpers had to milk the cows by hand, twice a day. Now electric milking machines are used, and two people are enough to operate them. The cows walk up the milking platform, the udders are washed with a sprayer, the milking machine is attached, and the milk flows through a hose into the pasteurizing machine.

"Shalom, Meir," I greet my friend.

"Shalom, Shmulek," he answers. "How many frogs did you catch last night?"

"Three of us caught twenty-eight of them in one evening," I tell him. Our best hunting grounds are around the cow sheds. We pack

the frogs into special tin boxes with holes for fresh air and lined with moss, and send them on the direct bus to the Hebrew University in Jerusalem, to the Biological Station there. The frogs are needed for experiments, and we are paid thirty grush for each frog.

"Your box of savings must be getting full," Meir says. "What do you do with all the money? You boys must have caught hundreds of frogs this month!"

"Two hundred and thirty-seven," I say. "And at our next group meeting we'll decide what to do with the money. I hope we'll vote to spend some of it on tickets for the circus from Austria that has come to Haifa."

"Why should you spend your savings for the circus?" Meir asks. "Surely the school pays for tickets?"

"Well, the school already paid when we went last week. The circus was really fabulous. It's the first time a circus has come to Israel, and we want to go again."

"I can understand that," says Meir.

Just then I see Yigal racing by in his tractor. He never drives at a normal speed, he always races.

"Stop, Yigal," I shout. "Please give me a lift!" He stops, and I climb into the wagon behind the tractor. Hagar and her friends from the vineyard are already in it. At lunch time Yigal and two other tractor drivers pick up all the people from the fields and orchards and bring them home.

In the village, everybody has stopped work and is walking to the dining hall. People come from the carpentry shop and from the workshop where plastic parts and cups and plates are made; from our lamp-shade factory they come, and from the chicken house; from the dressmaking room, and from the laundry. I see Yizchak the painter leave his work shack; and I meet the mechanics and shoemakers, and our landscape gardener. Everybody meets for the midday meal.

Yochevet calls to me from a kitchen window.

"Shmulek, come in, I have something you like very much!"

"What is it?"

"Come and see!" Yochevet answers. But first I look through the window. She is making k'tzetzot, chopped beefsteak patties, hundreds of them.

"Are they made of meat, or just extraordinary ones?" I ask. Everybody knows about Dollek's joke.

"No, not vegetable beefsteak," Yochevet answers, "real meat. I have already made three hundred." She gives me one, and it tastes delicious.

But now I must run, or I will be late for lunch at the Mosad.

On the lawn by the water tower the younger children are playing soccer. They do not live in the Mosad, but have their own place here. They have had their lunch already, earlier than the grownups, in their own dining hall.

For many years the water tower also served as our watch tower. It was the first structure in the village. In the years before Israel became the Jewish State, a guard was on the lookout all the time.

Before we had our own army, our village was often attacked by Arabs. All the men and women took turns watching the countryside from the tower, and they always had rifles with them.

On top of the water tower stands our Menorah, the eight-branched candelabra. Each winter, when we celebrate Hanukkah—the Feast of Lights—candles on the Menorah are lighted for eight nights. On Hanukkah we remember the battle of our forefathers under their leader Judas Maccabaeus and his brothers. More than two thousand years have passed since they fought for religious freedom and for national independence, and conquered Jerusalem back from the heathen.

After lunch, I work in the kitchen. Michael and Gideon and I dry two hundred ten forks, two hundred ten spoons, two hundred ten knives, one hundred five plates. And then come the cups, and I am really glad when we are finally finished. We go to our rooms and rest on our beds for an hour. This is the hottest time of the day, and a very good time to be lazy.

At two o'clock Doron and I go to the goat pen together. Right now we are both on duty there. We clean the pen and scrub the floor.

I bring fresh fodder and water for the goats. From outside, I hear the kids bleat, they know I am around, and I bring them their fodder and water too, and play a little with the kids.

Joseph comes and tells us to go milk the goats. Joseph is our instructor, he shows us how to do things on the farm. Every boy and girl in our children's community works in the afternoons, either in the fields, or in the vegetable and flower gardens, or with the animals. Every two months we change to another job, and that's how we learn everything a farmer has to know.

When we finish work, Joseph calls me over.

"Shmuel, please go to the village council at five o'clock, and ask whether boys and girls will be needed in the orchards again tomorrow. Poly wants to know."

Poly is the director of the Mosad. "I won't forget," I promise, and race over to the showers. I wash and change my clothes, and then I go to see my parents.

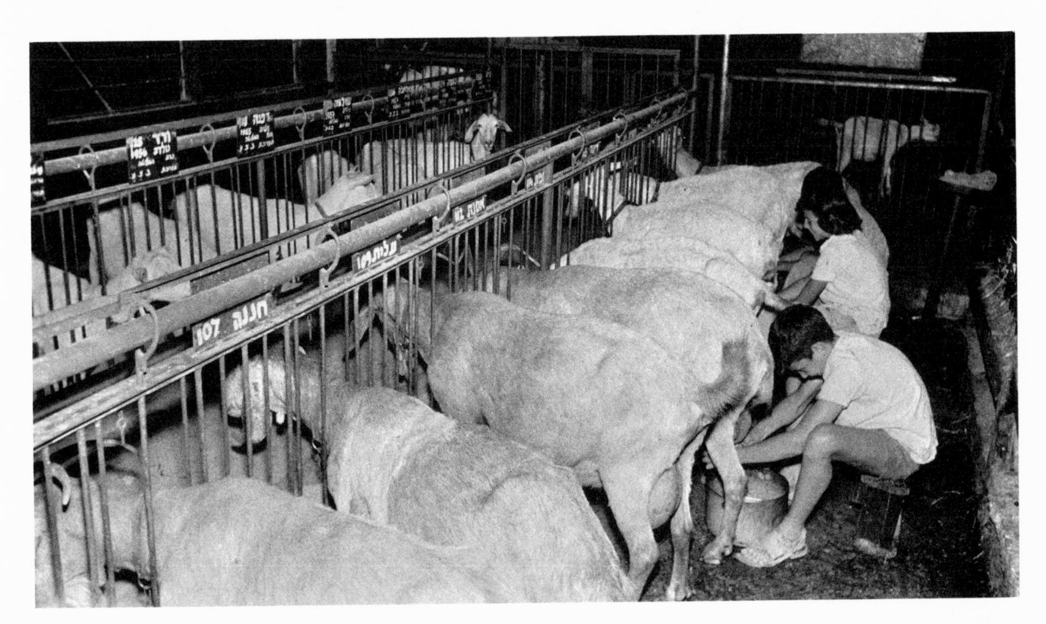

3

I walk around the big school building, where other groups live and study. I like it better where I live, because we have only four rooms and one classroom in our house.

Then I run along the palm-tree alley that leads down through the village to where my parents live. I try not to step on the shadows of the palm leaves. It isn't easy to do, the main thing is to take very small steps and at the same time to be very quick.

Abba and Imma live in one of the new houses behind the lawn. They have the left wing to themselves, with two rooms and a porch, and with a shower and toilet and a kitchenette. My parents always eat in the communal dining hall. But it is nice to be able to make coffee or tea at home in the afternoons and evenings or whenever friends drop in.

For twenty years, before Abba and Imma moved in here, they lived in one room, and they had a long walk to the showers. For the first five years after they came to Israel they lived first in a tent and then in a wooden shack. At that time there were only two concrete buildings in the whole village, one for the children and the other for the animals. And the watch tower, of course.

My parents are vatikim, old-timers; that's why, when the new houses were built, they were among the first ones to move into one of the two-and-a-half-room apartments.

They do not pay any rent, of course. Our village is a kibbutz, a collective settlement. In a kibbutz, all the property is owned by everybody in common. Nobody gets paid for the work he does, but nobody pays for anything he needs, either. Nobody needs money, the kibbutz pays for everything, except presents and special hobbies, and for these, every grownup gets an allowance of fifty pounds a year. The founders of the kibbutz were all friends, and they decided that this way of living together would please them most, and it would be the most practical too.

All the money that is earned goes directly into the village treasury. The general assembly of all chaverim decides how it should be spent.

They decide how much money is to go for new houses, for food, for machinery, for clothing and books and toys and entertainment. Last year we even built our own little hospital in the village.

Abba has planted flowers around the house, so I am careful to keep to the path and not to step on the lawn. I knock at the door, and Yuval shouts from inside:

"Come in, bulbul!"

"Shalom, Red Cap!" I say, when we shake hands. Every time he sees me, Yuval calls me by another bird name—to tease me, because I am a bird watcher.

"And do you mean the nightingale bulbul, or the noisemaker bulbul, Yuval? There are two kinds, as you should have learned!"

"Oh, I give up," says Yuval, "but I certainly wouldn't call you a nightingale, you bulbul."

"Both of you, stop teasing each other," says Imma. She has made coffee, and she brings out candy and cookies, and marmalade and bread. Adam has come with Abba. His parents and his smaller brother live in the town of Beer-Sheba, down south.

"When did you get your parachutist wings?" Abba asks.

"Last month," Yuval answers, "after the fifth jump. It was quite easy. But then I had to sew the wings on my uniform, all by myself, and *that* was hard, believe me."

"How you must have suffered, you poor boy." Now Imma herself can't help teasing my big brother.

"Yuval," I say, "I want to see you jump. Can't you smuggle me into the camp somehow?"

"You know, bulbul, you are a nudnik, a bother of the first order. . . . Here you are . . ." and he gives me a ticket, and another one to Adam. I look at mine—it is for the parachute-jump meet at Ashkalon.

"Oh, Yuval, how wonderful, you *are* a friend!" Adam is as excited as I am. "Will you jump too?" he asks.

"Sure I will, hundreds of us will jump. It will be a big affair. The President will be there, and the Prime Minister, and the Minister of Justice, and a couple of generals, and about twenty thousand other guests. That jump will be my farewell performance in the Army."

Every Israeli has to serve two years in the Army or in the Navy or Air Force, and every girl for eighteen months. Yuval's time will be over in two weeks, and then he will be back in the village for good.

"What are you boys going to do later?" Yuval asks us. "Shall we organize a basketball game?"

"I can't. I have to go to the council and ask about tomorrow. And then we're all going up to the old caravansary, we want to show it to Adam."

"Show Adam the third arch—I lived under it for a long time," Imma says.

Adam and I stuff ourselves with cookies and bread spread thick with marmalade, and then we go.

My sister Hagar and her husband Herzl are just coming for a visit, and little Daliya trips behind them with her friends. She tries to eat an orange whole, but it is much too big, of course. I draw her tambl hat a bit forward into her face.

"That's how big girls wear it," I tell her. But she gives me a suspicious look. She does not like *any* joke.

The meeting room of our village council is in the basement of the dining hall. The post office and the village telephone are there too.

Dollek is just putting stamps on the outgoing mail when we come in.

"Can I go into the meeting, Dollek?" I ask. "Did they decide about tomorrow? Do they need us?"

"They are making changes, Shmulek my friend," Dollek answers. "I have just come back from the weather station and I have told the council that we may have rain tomorrow afternoon. Rain would spoil the hay lying in the fields to dry."

"Isn't it a bit late for rain, Dollek?"

"No," Dollek answers. "We always have the last rain, the malkosh, in late spring, around Pesach."

"Last rain?" Adam asks now. "Do you mean it won't rain any more after that?"

"No," I tell him, "it won't. We never have any rain from about March until October or November."

"No rain for seven or eight months! Always a blue sky—but that's wonderful!" Adam exclaims.

"When the hot sharaw wind blows in from the desert I wish we had rain instead," I say.

I knock at the door to the council room and go in. Reuven sits at the head of the long table, he is the manager of all the farm work this year. Yigal is there too, and Siva, and Benyo.

"Shalom," I say. "Poly sent me to ask if you need us tomorrow for farm work."

"Yes, we do," Reuven answers. "Tell Poly we will need fifty children for thinning the corn. All the adults will be busy bringing in the hay. I'm sorry you won't have much time for dancing tonight—but that's up to Poly to decide. We expect you at five o'clock in the morning; please be on time."

"Shalom," I say, and I leave. Adam and I run to Poly's house to tell him the news. Poly makes a thoughtful face.

"You will be too tired tomorrow for a long trip, and we wouldn't be able to start in time—so what about our plan to go to Megiddo, boys? All right, we will still go, but we will do it one day later."

Most of my friends are already waiting in front of the dining hall. We sit on the lawn and fool around until everyone is there. Doron tries standing on his head like a circus acrobat, but he isn't good at it. I tell the group about tomorrow.

"Up at four thirty," says Elisheva, "how cruel." Elisheva can sleep for ten hours at a stretch, and she can get very rude if anybody wakes her.

"Let's go," Adam says. "We want to be back for the evening meal." Adam is always in time for meals, and I am too, to tell the truth; I love food.

We go down the gully behind the Mosad buildings, and cross over to the hill on the other side. Then we run up to our old oak tree. From the village, it looks small; but it is the biggest tree I ever saw.

"How old do you think the oak tree is, Adam?" I ask him.

"Everything old in Israel is *very* old," he answers, "I've found *that* out. I guess the tree is from Abraham's time, *at least*." Is he trying to pull my leg? I can't be sure, Adam is keeping a straight face.

"Not *that* old," says Uri, "but my father thinks it might be a thousand years old. In former times, whole caravans with all their camels sheltered in the shadow of the huge branches."

It is our favorite climbing tree. Once all of us children from the Mosad climbed up into the branches at the same time; we counted: there were one hundred and eighty-nine boys and girls.

We don't climb up the trunk, that would be impossible. But on the outer fringes the branches reach down to the ground, and we just walk up. Higher up, climbing becomes more difficult, but I climb on to my favorite seat, close to the top.

"Ouch!" I hear one of the girls cry out. It is Shulamit. She has jumped down from a low branch—and with her bare feet into a big thorn.

"It's a four-spiked one!" Yehiel calls. We have more than a hundred different kinds of thorns growing wild, but a four-spiked one is the worst kind to step into. It is very hard to get out again, and I climb down to help. Shulamit doesn't keep very still while we work on her foot. But a four-spiked thorn must be taken out at once, because it makes the foot swell.

"The thorn must have thought you were a horse!" Elisheva says.

"You're very flattering," Shulamit says angrily. "What makes you think so? You always know everything!"

"I learned it," Elisheva answers. "In Biblical times, four-spiked thorns were grown especially. They were thrown on the ground before the horsemen attacked, and were used as cavalry traps. It took only a few to make a horse limp."

"I am *not* a horse," says Shulamit. "Ouch! Ouch!"

"I got it!" Uri cries, and shows us the thorn.

"Thank you, Uri," Shulamit whimpers; her foot still hurts. She limps along with us, and we all go on now, down the hill and up the next one, to the ruins of the old caravansary.

"You better be careful next time," I warn Shulamit, "and don't jump from trees without looking where you're jumping."

"Thanks for the advice," she comes back at me, "I would rather step on a four-spiked thorn than on a snake, and that's what you did last year, Shmuel!"

"A real snake? Did it bite you?" Adam asks.

"It did, and then I killed it."

"Why didn't you die? Wasn't the snake poisonous?"

"Yes, it was. But it happened very near the village, and they immediately gave me an injection in the hospital. That saved me."

Only one side of the old caravansary is still standing. Many travellers used it for themselves and their animals for a night's rest, from the times of the Romans on.

I walk over with Adam to the third arch from the left. This is the

one Imma told me about. She and eleven others lived under these arches when they first came here. They were lucky to find this caravansary. They just covered the open sides with tent canvas, and the rooms were ready. And then they started draining the swamps down in the Valley of Jezreel.

I show it all to Adam, and we look down on our village from here, and on the Emek. Adam walks under the arch and calls from there:

"I don't see any electric wires! And where did they get water?"

"They had kerosene lamps. And there is a well two hundred yards away. That was the reason I think people built that rest house here in the first place."

"Are you sure your Imma lived under this arch?" Adam asks me.

"The third from the left, you heard her say so. This is it."

"This one is the third from the right," Adam answers. "Can't you count?"

"Nonsense," I say, and show him. "It is the third arch from the left."

"Nonsense yourself," says Adam. "Count from the right side!"

At last I see what he means. It is the third arch from the left *and* the third arch from the right at the same time. This time Adam really caught me.

The sun sinks over the ridge of Mount Carmel as we walk back to the village. Night falls very quickly in our country. A few minutes ago it was day, and now it is almost dark.

When we come to our house I switch on the verandah light. A swallow flies away.

"Look, Shmuel," says Uri, "the swallows are building their nest around the electric bulb. That's very clever."

"That's true," I say. "They have their nest heated by the bulb!"

As we watch, the swallow comes back, the light in the bulb does not disturb her at all. She carries a small lump in her short beak, and she adds it to the outside of the finished part of the nest.

"Why does it stick?" Adam asks me.

"The swallows mix a bit of clay or sand with spittle in their beaks. The spittle works like glue."

It is time to eat, and we go over to our dining hall. After the meal, Poly makes an announcement:

"Chaverim—friends—we have been asked to help with the corn and the hay tomorrow. We start out at five o'clock in the morning. Bedtime is nine o'clock tonight. Our hikes are postponed for a day. And now, everybody please help move the tables and chairs to the walls."

Uri and Moshe sit with their accordions in the middle of the hall, and Hanoch joins them with his trumpet. First they play "Kuma echa." We form a huge circle and hold hands, and we dance the hora and sing:

Kuma echa sov wasov,
Al tanucha shova shov. . . .

Get up, brothers, round and round,
Do not rest now, stand your ground.
Without start and without end
Do we dance now, hand in hand.

First we dance slowly. Then the musicians play faster and faster. A few of the dancers leave the circle, others join in quickly and take their places. The circle gets bigger and bigger, and a second one is formed inside the first one, until we all get out of breath and both circles break up. Then we sit around on the floor and sing.

Afterwards we dance again: polka and krakoviak and other folk dances.

Nine o'clock! We fool around a little while; then we go to our rooms, and wash, and go to bed.

The swallows are still working at their nest, sometimes two at the same time. Long after the lights are out I hear them swish through the air.

From the direction of the caravansary I hear the long, whimpering howl of a jackal. Our dog Felly answers with a sharp bark. He guards the ducks. I think he wants to let the jackal know he is here and ready for him. Another jackal starts howling. They are very noisy on moonlit nights, and tonight the moon is almost full.

The others are asleep already, I better get some sleep now too. I have to get up early tomorrow.

4

"Four thirty! Time to get up!"

This is Ofra, our house mother, waking us. She pulls the curtains aside to let the light in.

Who wants to get up so early! This is ridiculous!

"I didn't sleep a minute!" I complain. "I was bitten by every mosquito in the whole Emek. Look at my arms, Ofra!"

"If you were bitten by mosquitoes, one of you must have left the door open," Ofra answers.

"The mosquitoes didn't bite me!" Doron calls from his bed, and the other two in the room were not bitten either.

"Why did those wretched mosquitoes pick on me?" I ask angrily, but Ofra has no answer to that one.

"You must have very sweet blood," Doron teases me. "Mosquitoes love that."

I throw a pillow at him, and all four of us have a pillow fight before we jump out of bed.

It is already warm outside. The sun cannot penetrate the thick haze. There is a smell of desert sand. This will be a day of sharaw wind, it seems.

"Put your hats on," Ofra calls from the verandah. And then we trot down the palm-tree alley.

Herzl is already seated on his tractor, and our biggest flat trailer is coupled to it. There is room on it for fifty of us from the younger groups. We move off, and start singing our "Lazy Boy" song. We sing it as a three-part round:

Wake up, lazy boy!
Off to work we go.
Get up, get up,
Off to work we go.

Kookoorekoo, Kookoorekoo,
Loud the rooster crows—
Kookoorekoo, Kookoorekoo,
Loud the rooster crows!

"Must we always sing in Israel?" Adam asks. "I am still hoarse from last night. And I have a headache."

"You will have a much worse headache before the morning is over," I warn him. "Where is your tambl hat?"

"I hate hats," Adam answers. "They never stay on my head anyway, with all the hair I have."

"Why don't you get a haircut, then?"

"Because I like it this way," Adam comes back at me, "and I never needed a hat in Poland."

Willek sits behind us. He is going with us to show us what to do.

"The sun of Israel is not the sun of Poland, my friend," he says to Adam. "It burns very hard, and it is not healthy without a hat. Do you want a sunstroke? You are not used to our sun yet."

When the tractor stops we jump off and crowd around Willek.

"Now, friends," he says, "every one of you walks through a different furrow. Tear out all the small plants around the main plant."

"Ah, that makes for larger corn plants," Adam calls out.

"Are you already an expert on corn-growing?" Willek asks.

Adam laughs. "Yesterday, the little plums squeezed each other, today the little corn plants squeeze each other. What's the difference?"

Willek assigns us to the fields and we start to work. Ruth is on my left side; she is soon ahead of me. But Adam has never been in a cornfield before. Willek works with him, and shows him how to do it.

We work for two hours: bending down, pulling up, bending down, pulling up. My back starts aching, and I am glad when I see Herzl coming in a jeep. He brings milk, and bread and margarine and cheese, and baskets full of tomatoes and cucumbers and hard-boiled eggs. We sit around the jeep and have our meal.

After breakfast, we work for another hour. Then we crowd around Willek again. "You have done good work," he says. "I will tell you something: in three hours you've done what it would have taken me three full weeks to do by myself. Now you see what can be accomplished when all work together."

Herzl comes and drives us back again. Some of our chaverim stand in a field and investigate some handfuls of cut stalks.

"Did it work?" Willek calls over.

"Very well," David calls back.

"We planted a special mixture of peas and oats together in the same field," Willek explains to us. "And now we are testing a new harvesting machine from New Zealand. It cuts both peas and oats in such a way that they will dry at the same time. Until now, we had to grow peas and oats separately, and mix them later for fodder. It took up much more time."

Herzl has to drive over to the other fields to help getting in the hay, so we walk the last stretch.

We come to the tree nurseries. The first one is ours, the other one belongs to the Government. The saplings of all the fruit trees are cared for in the nurseries, before they are strong enough to be transplanted into the orchards.

The supervisor of the tree nurseries is Yulek, and there are always three or four others working with him. I see Isaiah with a big tank strapped to his back. He holds a sprayer in his hand. Aaron pumps, and a white liquid sprays down on the wild weeds on the ground.

"Shalom, children," the workers in the tree nursery call to us. We walk over and greet them. Aaron stops pumping. His sidecurls flutter in the wind. He came from the land of Yemen in Southern Arabia. Yemenite Jews are very religious. They always wear caps, and they grow beards and sidecurls.

Aaron and Isaiah live in a Yemenite village near Megiddo, and they work every day in the Government tree nursery.

"What are you spraying?" we ask Aaron.

"We use a mixture of oil and poisonous chemicals," he explains."It kills the parasite weeds on the ground. It's much easier than to rip the weeds out by hand. And over there, we are trying out a new variety of apples from Europe. It looks as if they would grow well here."

"Are you sure an apple tree from Europe will grow well here?" Adam asks. "It is used to other surroundings!"

We all listen to the talk now.

"I am sure, Adam," Aaron answers. "It takes time, of course, and a new plant must be given special care to feel comfortable and at home in a new place." He looks at Adam with a smile.

"Do you feel at home already in Israel, Adam, my friend? You have been here only two months."

"K'tzat," Adam says, "a little."

"You know, Adam, when I came here it wasn't so easy for me either at first. You just wait until you can speak Hebrew as well as your friends, that makes a lot of difference."

"Did you always work in a tree nursery, Aaron?" Adam wants to know.

"Oh, no, I was a potter in Yemen. We Jews were not allowed to be farmers there. There were only a few professions we could choose from. But here I am free, and I do what I have wanted to do all my life: I work on the land."

"You know, Adam, Aaron can read upside down," Elisheva says. "Isn't that true?"

Aaron laughs.

"I can read from every angle. There are no books printed in Yemen, and all we had were a few Bibles from Israel. When we learned to read, fifteen or more children shared one Bible with the teacher. He had the book in front of him, and we sat around in a semicircle on the floor. We had to read from wherever we sat. Try it yourself, you will get used to it too, I am sure. And now Shalom, children, I have to go back to work. Go in peace, and may the Holy One bless you."

"Shalom, Shalom," we call back, and then we walk on.

The barley stands high, it is already yellow and ripe. The sheaves sway back and forth in the wind. It looks pretty. Tomorrow, we will begin our Pesach festival with the ceremony of cutting the first sheaves of barley from this field. The cypress trees farther off have been planted as windbreakers for the groves beyond. The orange trees and grapefruit and lemons grow better if they are sheltered from the wind.

We hurry on and come to the village. Uri's father, Emanuel, stands near the sheep and goat pens. He is talking to Shafik. I know Shafik, he is an Arab Israeli from Nazareth. Uri and Adam and I walk over, but the others go on, back to the Mosad.

"Shalom, veladim," Shafik greets us in Hebrew, "Peace be with you, boys!"

"Shalom, Shafik," we answer, and Uri asks in Arabic:

"Keef Khalak!" It means, "How are you?" Shafik answers in Hebrew again. He knows it very well, and we know quite a bit of Arabic.

Shafik has come over to buy a few goats, he says.

"Where does Shafik come from?" Adam wants to know, and we tell him.

"Nazareth? Is Nazareth near our village?"

"Of course it is. Didn't you know?" And we point to the hills of Galilee across the Valley of Jezreel. "Over there, where the smoke rises above the ridge."

"Is that the Nazareth where Jesus lived with his parents? I learned about it, back in my school in Poland."

Shafik has heard our talk. He smiles with his many golden teeth.

"Yes, my friend, I live in the Nazareth you have heard about," he tells Adam. "My house is not far from Mary's Well. When you come and visit me with your friends, you will see the women stand in line

for water at that well just as they did at the time when Jesus was a boy. But you have to come soon, because we have a new water system at last. Many houses already have modern plumbing, and the water comes mostly through the pipes now."

"Thank you for the invitation," we say, and we promise to visit Shafik during our vacation.

"Boys, could you help me in the woods after lunch today?" Emanuel asks. "I have to hack out some weeds."

Adam can't come, he has his Hebrew lessons, but Uri and I are pleased that Emanuel will take us with him.

Emanuel is in charge of the farm buildings now. For many years he was our chief forester, and he has planted more trees than anybody else in our woods. But now the trees are grown, and there is little for Emanuel to do in the forest.

But Emanuel always finds a reason to visit his beloved trees.

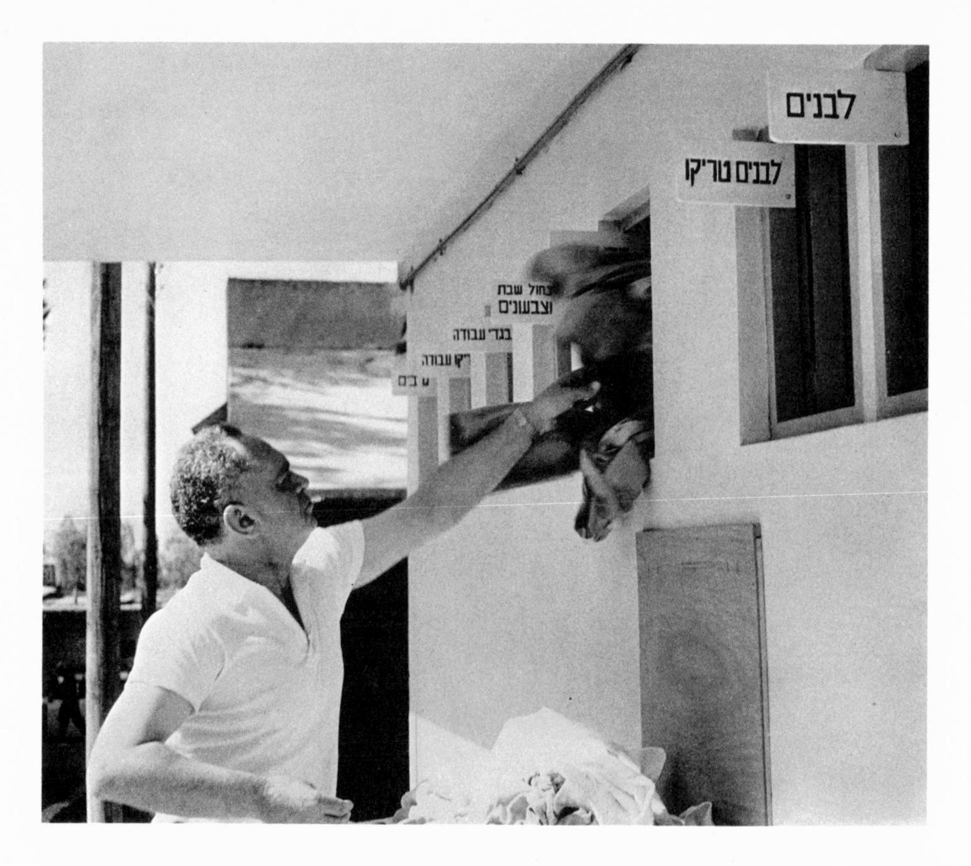

"Get out the two-wheeled cart after lunch," he tells us now. "I will come to the shed with the horse and with the tools."

We say Shalom to Emanuel and Shafik, and go to our rooms. I throw myself on my bed. I *am* tired. Now is a good time to make up for the sleep we didn't get last night.

5

Uri wakes me in time for lunch and afterwards we walk to the cart sheds. Doron goes to the goats, he will take them down to the big sheds in the village for me.

On the way we pass the laundry house. Uri's uncle Dodya is just throwing his laundry through the open windows in the wall. Each window has a sign to tell where to throw what: there are separate windows for blouses, underwear, working clothes, Sabbath clothes, white shirts, sheets, socks, towels, handkerchiefs. The chaverim bring their laundry here every week, and pick up their clean things.

"Have you heard about our basketball team?" Dodya asks us. "I heard the news a few minutes ago on the radio."

"What happened?" Uri asks. His brother Amos is the best player in the country, and we play basketball almost every day.

"Our team will play in the finals!" Dodya says.

"Wonderful!" we shout. We are sure we will win the championship this year.

At the sheds, we get out the small two-wheeled cart. Emanuel comes with the horse Serafa. He carries three turiahs over his shoulder, the shovel axes for working the ground.

We tell him the great news about our basketball team, and he promises to come to the game with us.

We harness Serafa to the cart. Emanuel takes the reins. There is just enough room for Uri and me to squeeze in behind him.

"Hoyah!" Emanuel calls, and old Serafa pulls us forward.

The road leads up the long alley of cypress trees, and then we come to the woods.

"Eucalyptus trees—cypress trees—pine trees—what a wonderful scent!" Emanuel says and sniffs the air. "I will tell you something, boys. We plant trees for many reasons: for one, so that the winter rains can't wash the soil away and erosion stops, and the land becomes more fertile. And then, the climate gets better when there are woods. And of course we can have our own timber. We even make our own furniture in the village from the timber we cut here.

"But what I like best about our woods is their beauty, and the shady walks, and the many birds we now have . . . and of course, the scent, the scent in the air!

"Hoyah! Hoyah!" Emanuel spurs Serafa on to a faster trot. Her name means fire, but she doesn't run at all like fire, she is very slow.

"Why was Serafa given that name?" I ask. "She is a bit slow, isn't she?"

"Serafa is very old now," Emanuel says. "Don't you know how she got her name? Listen:

"It was on a blisteringly hot afternoon, many years before you two were born. The sharaw was blowing hard that day.

"I was working up here, with two friends. Suddenly I smelled smoke and heard the crackling noise of burning twigs.

" 'Fire!' I shouted, 'Fire! Fire!' We ran up the slope over there, and then we saw it: the forest on the west side was burning.

"We raced down to the village. Many people, with wet sacks over their shoulders, were already running toward us, to the woods. They had seen the fire, and came to fight it.

"I ran to the horse stable. We had only two horses at that time. One of our chaverim was out with one, guarding the fields. So I had to take the other one, although I knew she was soon to have a foal.

"We harnessed the horse to a cart, and in the cart we threw sacks which we had dipped in water. Then we put three barrels of water on the cart, and drove uphill to the woods as fast as the mare could pull. A few hundred yards from the forest I left her in the meadow, and from there we ourselves pulled the cart with the wet sacks and the water barrels.

"There were more than a hundred of us up here by then, trying to stop the fire. We dug a shallow ditch a few hundred yards in front of it. When the fire crept close, we struck at the flames and the sparks with our wet sacks, so they would not reach the other side of the ditch.

"We fought the fire for hours, until there was no strength left in our arms. Our faces were black with soot and ashes, and we could hardly breathe because of the heat and the thick smoke.

"At last we got the fire under control—it did not spring over the ditch, and it burned itself out. But more than thirty thousand trees were burned to the ground in a few hours. The earth was pitch black, and only charred stumps were left of the beautiful trees. It was horrible to see. I think I cried.

"After the fire was out I went back to the mare. There I saw something black lying on the grass, stretching its legs. A foal! A foal was born up here, all alone, while the fire was raging.

"We will call you Serafa, I said to the foal—Fire—because you were born when our trees were on fire."

Emanuel pulls on the reins, and Serafa stops. We take the tools and start working. We hack out wild growth around the trees, and pull out the weeds with their roots.

"This is not just undergrowth and brush," Emanuel tells us, "these are parasite plants. They live off the trees, and make them rot."

We take the parasite plants back with us to the village. They must be burned, or they will take root again and harm the trees.

"Hey," I say. "I just felt some drops on my face! The malkosh!" The same moment it starts raining hard.

"So Dollek's prediction was right," Uri says.

"A good thing he warned us," Emanuel replies. "I think the hay is in by now. How many boys and girls from the Mosad went out to help with the hay?"

"About a hundred," Uri tells him. "Another fifty of us went to the cornfields, and the others were needed on the farm and in the kitchen." We get quite wet—not that I mind it. I like getting wet. It is fun to work in the woods when it rains.

Last winter we often came to the woods when it rained. Almost every day we went mushroom picking, and we children from the Mosad collected over two thousand pounds in three months.

Emanuel has spotted something, and we go over to have a close look: it is a cluster of pink cyclamen flowers, growing in the shade of a boulder.

"You see, boys, even cyclamen grow here now that we have a forest. These will be the last ones this year."

"Why the last ones, Abba?" asks Uri.

"Cyclamen never grow after the malkosh," Emanuel answers. "They cannot stand the heat that comes after the last rain. They just wither and die, they are very delicate plants."

"Abba," says Uri, "don't the cyclamen have another name, also? Aren't they also called Solomon's Crown?"

"I have heard that told by my grandmother, long ago, when I was a child, back in Russia—but I can't remember."

"I know the story," I say. "Our Nature teacher told us about it."

"Tell us, Shmulek," says Emanuel.

"It was like this: When Solomon became king, he wanted a special design for his crown. But he didn't like any of the designs the artists brought to him. One day, he walked in his flower garden. His eyes fell on a bunch of pink cyclamen that were growing in a remote spot. Their petals looked exactly like a crown, and they were arranged in just the shape he had had in mind. That was the design he had wanted.

"So King Solomon commanded his artisans to make him a crown in the same shape, and from then on the cyclamen got its second name, King Solomon's Crown."

We drive back again through the rain to the village, old Serafa pulling us slowly along.

After the evening meal I practice on my trumpet. Yuval gave it to me as a present. My favorite tune is an American song about a soldier who comes from Alabama with a banjo on his knee.

I have to blow hard to get a decent tone out of my trumpet; sometimes it squeaks.

Doron and the others lie on their beds and stop their ears with their hands and read. They don't like it when my trumpet squeaks. But I think they overdo it; anyway, I don't play that badly.

Ofra comes in and says, "Be careful tonight with the door, or the mosquitoes will bite you again, Shmuel."

"Ofra, does the whole Mosad go to Megiddo tomorrow?" Doron asks. "All one hundred and eighty of us?"

"Oh, no," Ofra answers. "One group goes to Haifa, to visit a ship in harbor, I think it is the *Jerusalem* that came in today. And another group goes to Mount Tabor, and then to the Nesher cement plant."

"Poly said he is coming with our group," I tell my friends. "First we'll go up to Elijah's monument, and then to Megiddo Fortress."

When we get ready for bed, I make sure the door is closed properly. I don't want any more insect bites!

6

After breakfast, three of our big open trucks pull up at our dining hall. We climb into the third one. Yizchak starts the engine and off we go. We all stand in the truck, and hold on tight to the sides.

There is much traffic on the road to Haifa today. The buses are full, and at the stops I see waiting crowds. Many people from the cities and villages spend the Pesach days with their relatives and friends in the country, it's a custom. And they all travel today.

Everybody carries a bundle, or a briefcase, or a child, or a chicken, and many men and women are already dressed in their best clothes.

After we pass the village of Yokneam, we turn left into a valley, and then we have a bumpy drive up to the Carmel ranges. The road passes between olive trees and vineyards. Poly tells us that olive oil from these mountains was already being exported by King Solomon. And the word Carm-El, if you take it apart, means Vineyard of God. The ancient Hebrews chose that name because the wine from here has always been the best in the country.

The truck stops, and we walk through stony meadows; they are covered with oleander bushes, and wild flowers blossom between the boulders. We come to an opening, and there, in front of a monastery, stands a huge statue of the Prophet Elijah, a dagger raised high in his right hand, one foot on the back of a man lying on the ground. I think it must be one of the heathen priests Elijah defeated.

We all know something about Elijah, but nobody knows all of it, so we sit on the steps of the monument and Poly helps us piece the story together.

"Many people believe that right here the Prophet Elijah met the heathen priests in that famous contest."

Yizchak has left the truck and come with us. He adds: "Elijah lived in the ninth century before Jesus, during the reign of King Ahab and the wicked Queen Jezebel. Where would you find the story?"

"If it happened during the reign of a king, it must be in the Book of Kings," says Uri, and we all laugh because it's so simple.

"Elijah was always fighting against the worship of idols," Poly says. "After his death, many legends were told about him; do you know one of them?"

"I remember the story now," says Gideon. "The name of the heathen god was Baal. He had about four hundred and fifty priests. Elijah challenged them all to a contest up here. Two bullocks were slaughtered. The Baal priests chose one and laid it on their altar on top of dry wood, but they did not put fire to it. And Elijah took the second bull and did the same on *his* altar. And then . . ."

Poly has brought a Bible along. He gives it to Gideon, who soon finds the passage. "First Book of Kings," he says, "chapter 18, verse 24: 'And call you on the name of your god, and I will call on the name of the Lord; and the God who answers by fire, let him be God.' "

Gideon closes the book but he keeps his finger between the pages. "The Baal priests called all morning on their god, but no fire came down on their altar."

"That's when Elijah made fun of them," I interrupt, and Gideon opens the Bible again and recites from it: "And Elijah mocked them, and said: 'Cry aloud; for he is a god; either he is musing, or he is gone aside, or he is on a journey, or perhaps he is asleep, and must be awaked.' About noon, the heathen priests gave up, and then it was Elijah's turn. He said: 'O Lord, God of Abraham, Isaac and Israel, let it be known this day that You are God in Israel. Answer me, O God, answer me.'

"And then a fire fell from heaven on Elijah's altar and consumed the sacrificial bull and, the legend says, the fire devoured even the altar itself. And that was the end of idol worshipping in that time."

We go over to the monastery, and pull at the bell. A monk comes out and greets us, and he invites us to look at the gardens.

From there we have a grand view. The Valley of Jezreel is dotted with white stone houses.

"Who lives in all those villages down there?" Adam asks. "Are they all kibbutz settlements like ours?"

"Oh no," Poly tells him. "There are different kinds of villages in Israel. In many of them, everybody owns the house where he lives with his whole family, and he owns his own animals and his own land, and works for himself only. But the big machinery for harvesting and the dairy are owned by all the people in the village. They would be too expensive for one farmer alone."

We sit down in the shade of the olive trees.

"The trees here are not very old," the monk tells us, "but on the other side we have trees that are over two hundred years old, and we still get very fine olives from them."

"Do trees really grow as old as that?" Adam asks. He still does not quite believe what we told him about our old oak tree at home.

"Oh yes," says the monk. "In the Garden of Gethsemane, just outside Jerusalem, there are some olive trees that are even older than ours. People think they are the descendants of the olive trees Jesus and his disciples saw. You know, before an olive tree dies it often sends up new shoots from the ground."

"In the time of ancient Israel," Poly tells us, "there was an oil press in that garden, that's what the word Gethsemane means."

We have several hundred olive trees in our groves, but they are not nearly so old. We harvest them in winter, and all year around we have olives on the table. I love them, but when Adam first ate one he spit it out and made a face.

"It tastes horrible," he exclaimed. "Like cherries dipped in herring sauce! Ugh!" But now he likes them and eats them all the time. We have a saying: The newcomer who gets used to olives will love the land.

"Olive trees are so beautiful," says Elisheva. "Look at the leaves, blue-green on the upper side, and silvery white underneath. And when the wind mixes the colors don't they look like silk?"

"Take cover!" Uri shouts. "Elisheva is getting poetic!" But he doesn't mean it really, what Elisheva said is quite true.

Yizchak looks at his watch and says, "If you still want to go to Megiddo, we better leave now." We shake hands with the monk, and say Shalom, and then we go to our truck.

On the drive back, we pass our village. After ten more minutes on the highway, Yizchak stops and lets us off, and then he leaves us.

A signpost in Hebrew and English points to the village of Megiddo. The ancient fortress of Megiddo is a mound that rises up a bit farther away, and we walk toward it.

"What do you think is in the hill in front of us?" I ask Adam. I have not been inside Megiddo yet myself, but I wrote about the tell of Megiddo on my test two days ago, and I know all about it.

"Inside that hill there, with the chopped-off top?" Adam asks. "Earth, I suppose, with a few worms mixed in, and rocks."

"Yes," I say, "and about twenty destroyed cities, one built on top of the ruins of the previous one."

"And heaps of strange cactus berries, I suppose!" Adam laughs. He doesn't trust me much since Uri and I played that trick on him.

"It isn't a hill at all," Poly says. "It is an artificial mound, a tell. Thousands of years ago, people of the stone age built a settlement there, right at the level of the plain. At some later time this settlement was destroyed. After a while, a new one was built on top of the

rubble of the first one. During the next few hundred years, the second settlement was destroyed, and the third, and the fourth, and so on.

"Every time a new town, with walls around it, was built on the remains of the destroyed one. And that way the place grew higher and higher, until now it looks like a hill with a flat top.

"And now all of you listen, friends! Thirty years ago, American archeologists started digging down from the top into the hill. They excavated the four top layers of the rubble and found the remains of four ancient walled cities.

"You can imagine their excitement, when in the fourth layer they found the remains of a fortress built by King Solomon! Come with me and I will show you something!"

We walk up a stone-paved ramp. Then we balance along old walls, and wander among the excavated grounds.

We crowd around Poly, and he explains.

"Look up there to the left, where the palm tree stands, and then up to the right, where those bushes grow. Now imagine a line leading from the palm tree to the bushes. Before the archeologists came about thirty years ago, the tell reached up to that level. Everything below it has been excavated during the last thirty years, and we are really standing inside the mound.

"Do you see the three levels on the rubble wall over to the right? Each one is a separate layer, each one is the rubble remains of an ancient town. The courtyard below us is in the fourth layer—it was once the courtyard of a house within the fortress enclosure of King Solomon. And the ramp we just walked up was used by King Solomon's charioteers, when they drove back here from an outing—or from a battle."

The very chariots of King Solomon came up here! This is exciting!

"Why did King Solomon and all the other people before him build a fortress just at this spot?" one of us wants to know.

"Look through the opening in the tell and you will understand the reason. On the other side of the valley there are more hills. The Valley of Jezreel was a famous throughway between Asia in the North and Egypt in the South.

"The caravans and armies from Syria, and from ancient Babylonia and Persia came down south from the right. The caravans and armies from Egypt came from the left, and they all met, peacefully or in war, right in this valley.

"Whoever held Megiddo up here dominated the passage through the Valley of Jezreel."

We walk on and come to rows of low stone pillars sticking up from the ground.

"Here were the stables," says Poly. "King Solomon had more than four hundred horses in the fortress. And over there were the buildings for a hundred and fifty chariots."

"Did they find dead horses?" Amram wants to know.

"No, I don't think so," Poly answers. "But they found hundreds of ivory carvings, and jewelry, and game boards, and necklaces, and thousands of ancient jars and shards."

"Perhaps we can find some rings or carvings too," Adam suggests, and we start digging with our hands at a rubble wall.

Adam gives a shout. "I've found a nail from a chariot!" he yells. He has an old rusty piece of iron that could really have been one.

I pull out a piece of brownish pottery, and Uri gets another like it.

"These are nice parts from ancient jars," Poly says. "Take them along to our museum." We find a few more broken pieces, and then we go on until we come to a deep pit in the ground, walled with stones.

"This was a grain cellar, probably for the barley or oats they stored in the fortress of King Solomon," Poly tells us. "It is a silo just like the ones we have in the village. We build ours above ground, and this one was built below ground, but they both serve the same purpose."

We walk down the steep stone steps, and have a good look at the ground. But we don't find any remains of ancient times.

"Come up," Doron shouts down to us, "we're going to climb the fortress walls!"

Poly again explains.

"The masons of the time of King Solomon made the wall here of huge stones cut from the rock, putting them on top of each other without mortar."

"Are we standing on the same wall where King Solomon himself once stood?" we ask.

"Perhaps. But certainly his captains and his charioteers stood here and looked over to Mount Tabor." Poly raises his stick and points to it. Mount Tabor looks near from here, with its rounded shape and the monastery at its summit.

To the left we see the Kishon River run its course to the Mediterranean coast.

"Remember, we talked about the battles fought in the Valley of Jezreel, between here and the foot of Mount Tabor," Poly says. "One of the biggest battles was fought near the Kishon River by ancient Hebrew tribes under the leadership of the Prophetess Deborah and her general, Barak. That was more than a hundred years before Solomon became king.

“Sisera, the general of the Canaanites, made war on the Hebrew tribes. He assembled nine hundred iron chariots for the big attack. The Hebrew tribes had no chariots at all at that time.

“Deborah had a plan. Together with Barak, she assembled ten thousand men in the woods of Mount Tabor. From there, they watched the enemy's chariots advance across the dried-up river bed into the Valley of Jezreel.

“They waited and waited. Then it happened. A thunderstorm broke out and torrents of rain came down. The chariot wheels and the horses of the Canaanites got stuck in the mud. And now the Hebrew tribes attacked. The chariots were unable to recross the Kishon River. The torrents of water swept them away. Sisera's army was completely routed by the pursuing Hebrews. They won the day on the banks of the Kishon.

“This was the decisive battle against the Canaanites. Sisera was killed, and from then on there was peace in the country for many, many years.”

We climb down from the fortress. At the foot of the Megiddo mound the daisies stand high in the fields. We pick armfuls of flowers for the Pesach Festival tonight.

Back on the highroad, we start walking toward our village. But it has become very hot, and we decide to hitchhike. We stop every truck and ask for lifts. Each one has room for two or three of us.

"We will meet at the museum," Poly tells us. He and Adam and I get the last lift, on a dairy truck.

We take the flowers to the kitchen and stand them in pails of water. Later they will be arranged on the tables. Then we go to our museum, behind Poly's house, on the way to the woods.

Poly takes Adam's ancient nail and all the potsherds we others have found and places them on a special shelf.

"When school starts again," he says, "you can find out from your teacher from which period your pieces date. And then you will report your finds to the Archeological Museum in Jerusalem. Perhaps we will be allowed to keep them in our museum."

Most of the pieces in our museum were found on our own grounds. When the land behind the Mosad was levelled to make a big athletic field, ancient burial places were found in the soil, and we dug up beautiful vases and jars and slingshots from three thousand years ago. What we find on our own land we are allowed to keep in our own museum.

Every piece we find we put there, and we write on a little card when it was found and where, and which period we think it is from.

7

After the midday rest, we meet our friends on the verandah of the big Mosad building and stand around and talk—about Megiddo, and about our basketball team.

Now Adam wears a hat, when it isn't necessary at all.

We play basketball, and then I take a shower and dress for the festivities in a white shirt and blue shorts. The girls in my group change from their shorts into long white dresses with long, full sleeves and blue trimmings. Then Adam and I go to see my parents.

Abba and Imma are home, and Yuval is there too. I have made a dovecote from an orange box. Yuval and Adam help me put it up in the nut tree. The pigeon keeper over at the village of Hazoreah has promised me four pigeons: two white ones and two brown ones. Tomorrow Adam and I will go over and get them.

Abba calls from the porch: "Time to go!" He and Yuval wind red sashes around their waists; Imma puts on her best embroidered blouse. Together we walk over to the dining hall.

The whole village is gathering there. Only the babies and their nurses stay home.

When all are together we go down to the fields for the ceremony of the cutting of the first sheaves. The Pesach Festival starts.

First march the reapers, carrying their scythes over the shoulders. With them go their oldest sons and daughters. The sons help them reap, the daughters do the gleaning. Uri's father leads, and Uri's sister and brother follow close behind.

After the reapers comes an open wagon. The little children and the band ride in it. Behind the wagon walk the dancers in their long white dresses. And then come all the rest of us.

The music plays, and we sing:

> Shuru habitu uréu . . .
>
> See, and look, and behold
> How great is this day . . .

Adam and I walk with Imma. Adam asks her, "Ruth, I know we celebrate Pesach tonight because it was at this time of year that Moses led our forefathers out of Egypt and they became free people. But what has that got to do with cutting the first barley?"

"Nothing except the time," Imma answers. "Pesach really combines two celebrations. You know all about the Exodus from Egypt. At about the same time of the year the first barley is ripe in the fields, and the young calves and the kids and the lambs are born. Pesach is also our spring festival, and that is why we walk together to the fields and cut the first barley and dance and sing."

When we come to the fields, we sit on the ground around them. The reapers swing their scythes and cut the sheaves. The gleaners follow behind, gather the sheaves, and bind them into bundles.

The reapers work their way through the field with dashing strokes. It does not take long before the first field is harvested.

The reapers stand aside now, and the gleaners carry their bundles in their outstretched arms and put them down before the people. And now the dancers stand up. My cousin Loga is among them and so are five others from my group.

First they stand still and raise their arms solemnly toward the sky. Then they begin the round dance of Spring. They move to and fro, and some of them kneel while others dance around them with outstretched arms.

Michael accompanies the dancers on his shepherd's drum. Then two mouth organs take over and an accordion and a trumpet, and we all sing:

Artza Aleenu . . .

We came to our land
And we have ploughed
And we have sown
And now we'll reap the harvest. . . .

The sun is disappearing behind the Carmel ridges, and we walk slowly back home.

In the dining hall the meal is on the tables, and there are flowers everywhere. Instead of bread we have matzah today, thin crusty squares, like crackers, made of flour and water.

Over a hundred people sit at each of the seven long tables. Six hundred people are from our village and the others are guests from all over the country. We sit on chairs, on benches, and on orange crates.

Yizchak the painter has painted the murals on the walls. They show scenes from the life of Moses, and how he led the ancient Israelites from Egypt to the Promised Land. Other panels show how people in our own time have come from many lands to Israel, and how we work the land as free people.

When everybody is seated the doors open, and ten girls walk through the rows of tables to the front. They carry the newly cut barley sheaves high above their heads, and lay them down on the stage. The choir sings:

Come to the fields and
Look at the vineyards,
See how everything blossoms and grows.

The rains are gone and
The dew is coming
See how everything blossoms and grows.

Everybody has a book with the Haggadah, the story of Pesach, in front of him. Ben Ami leads us in reading it aloud. He always prepares the programs for our festivals. Now he speaks:

"Why do we eat this matzah today? Because when our forefathers left Egypt they had no time to wait until the leaven would make the dough rise. They had no time to linger."

And he goes on to say that there was no time to bake proper bread. Instead, flour and water was mixed and without yeast or salt quickly baked into the matzah flatbread. In memory of this, every year, on the night of the full moon of this month of Nissan, we celebrate the Exodus from Egypt, and eat matzah as our forefathers did.

Ben Ami calls on different people to recite passages from the book. In our Haggadah are many new passages which have to do with life in our villages. When Ben Ami calls on little Hagar, she stands up on her chair. She is only five years old, and she shouts her lines into the hall. "Why is this night different from all other nights? Because on other nights the children eat separately, but tonight we all eat together with our parents!" And she adds, "Except the babies."

Everybody bursts out laughing.

Between the readings the choir sings, and then the meal starts. It is just about the biggest meal we have all year.

After the meal, the dance group of our kibbutz come on the stage. With every step they take, the dancers shake the tambourines in their hands, and the little cymbals in the tambourines tinkle.

I leave my place and meet my friends on the verandah behind the stage. There we dress quickly in old rags for the pantomime we are going to perform.

Loga wraps herself in a goatskin, she is going to play a kid. I put on a dog's mask and Uri a cat's mask. We made them in the workshop out of stiff wrapping paper.

Adam carries a long stick, and Shulamit gets a poster with FIRE written on it. Amram takes a water kettle, and Gideon fastens two cows' horns on his head to play the ox. Elisheva dresses up in a sheet, with paper wings on her shoulders. Doron is going to play the butcher.

We line up on the stage. Ofra sits at the piano and gives the sign. Yigal steps to the front, he is our narrator. He drums out a rhythm on his goatskin drum, and sings the verses. And now we start to act out the last song in our Pesach book as a pantomime, while Yigal begins the first verse in a loud voice:

"One only kid, one only kid my father bought for two farthings."

Loga in her goatskin hobbles around on the stage and bleats loudly.

"Then came the cat that ate the kid," Yigal sings on.

Uri the cat jumps on the stage and starts nibbling at Loga.

"Then came the dog that bit the cat. . . ."

That's me, and I bite Uri's shoulder. "Hey," he says, "don't be so realistic!" But I hang on until he flees down the back of the stage, and I bark triumphantly like a real dog who has won a fight. But Yigal sings:

"Then came the stick that beat the dog. . . ."

Adam runs up to me, and he *does* beat me with his long stick until I run away. He overdid it, I will pay him back later.

We are a big success, everybody in the crowd laughs at our acting. Yigal has to shout to make himself heard:

"Then came the fire that burned the stick. . . ."

At these words, Shulamit hits Adam over the head with the FIRE poster and he rolls on the ground with goggling eyes exactly as we rehearsed it. Shulamit displays the poster proudly, and the story goes on:

"Then came the water that quenched the fire. . . ."

At this point Amram pours water over the word FIRE on the poster and over Shulamit's bowed head, as if she were a flowerpot. It looks so funny we howl with laughter. Gideon now trots slowly onto the stage, with the cows' horns on his head:

"Then came the ox that drank the water. . . ." Yigal recites.

Amram pours water into Gideon's open mouth, and when the kettle seems empty he turns it upside down for the last drops to come out, and Gideon licks them up. But Amram sits down and pretends to have fainted.

"Then came the slaughterer who killed the ox. . . ."

Doron goes after Gideon and taps him gently on the head with a toy hammer. Gideon the ox falls like dead to the ground.

Now it gets serious. Yigal sings with a solemn voice:

"Then came the angel of death who slew the slaughterer. . . ."

Elisheva comes walking on in her white sheet. She waves her wand over Doron and that is the end of *him*. Doron falls down. Only the angel remains. Yigal goes on:

"Then came the Holy One, blessed be He, who smote the angel of death."

The angel walks away as if in a dream, and the stage is empty. And now Yigal sings the song again, from the last verse backwards. He sings it faster and faster, and everybody in the dining hall joins in the song:

"He smote the angel of death who slew the slaughterer who killed the ox that drank the water that quenched the fire that burned the stick that beat the dog that bit the cat that ate the kid my father bought for two farthings, for two farthings!"

Our Pesach celebration always ends with this song. After that we all move the tables and benches and chairs and orange crates to the walls. Two chaverim bring their accordions and the dancing begins. First, the hora is danced in big circles, and then come the polka and the krakoviak in fours and twos.

When we return to the Mosad it is long after midnight. The full moon shines in the clear sky between the cypress trees. I see the whole Emek in its gleam. A few lights glitter in the valley. All is quiet now in my village.

GLOSSARY

Chaverim	means "friends." The members of our village are called *chaverim,* when they are boys or men. But when they are girls or women, they are called *chaverot.*
"Ein davar"	"It does not matter!"
Grush	is a coin, and one hundred grush make one Israeli pound, which is worth about fifty cents.
Haifa	is the biggest port in Israel.
Hanukkah	Our Feast of Light. We celebrate it in December.
Hora	is our national dance. We dance it in a huge circle.
Jerusalem	is the capital of Israel. It is the seat of the Government, and of the Parliament.
Jordan	Our main river.
Kibbutz	A collective settlement, like our village. There are three hundred collective settlements in Israel. In a kibbutz everything belongs to everybody, and everybody has the same rights and the same duties.
"K'tzat"	"A little."
K'tzetzot	Chopped meat patties.
"Maher!"	"Quick!"
Malkosh	is the last rain in spring, before the long hot summer begins. In summer it doesn't rain for seven or eight months at a stretch.
Matzah	The thin crusty unleavened flatbread we eat at Pesach.
Menorah	The eight-branched candelabrum we light on Hanukkah.
Nudnik	is what you call somebody who is a big brother.
Pesach	The Passover Festival, when we celebrate the Exodus from Egypt. It was then that Moses led our forefathers to the Promised Land. On this day falls also our Spring Festival, when the first sheaves of barley are cut.
Sabra	The wild cactus fruit in our country. Everybody born in Israel is also called a Sabra.
"Shalom"	"Peace."
Shamenet	Sour cream. I like it with scallions and green pepper and tomatoes cut into it.
Sharaw	The dry hot wind that blows in from the desert.
Tambl	means a sort of simpleton. Everybody looks a bit like a tambl in the special sun hat we wear. That's why we call them tambl hats.
Tinok	Baby.
Vatikim	are the old-timers in our village, like my parents.
"Yaféh"	"Beautiful!"
Yotzeh min haklal	means "extraordinary."

Maps by Anne Marie Jauss